poyums

poyums

Len
Pennie

CANONGATE

First published in Great Britain, the USA and Canada in 2024 by
Canongate Books Ltd, 14 High Street, Edinburgh EH1 1TE

canongate.co.uk

Distributed in the USA by Publishers Group West
and in Canada by Publishers Group Canada

5

British Library Cataloguing-in-Publication Data
A catalogue record for this book is available on
request from the British Library

ISBN 978 1 80530 138 7

Typeset in Bembo by
Palimpsest Book Production Ltd, Falkirk, Stirlingshire

Printed and bound by CPI Group (UK) Ltd, Croydon CR0 4YY

Fur Jimmy Pennie, Jean Davidson,
Bert Davidson an Nancy Mclaren.
Aye mindit, aye thankit, aye mist.

Contents

Introduction

I'D LOVE TO SAY my writing process was smooth and easy, that I had a plan and a structure in mind, but I didn't. Most of the pieces were written in pain and in solitude, me on my phone on my bathroom floor trying desperately to find a healthy way to deal with my emotions. I'm sorry there aren't more happy pieces, but then again, I'm sorry there weren't more happy times to write about.

It is an incredible privilege for me to be able to write and publish in the Scots language, and I want to acknowledge the struggle and sacrifice that made this possible. This book is for every person who was told the way they spoke was wrong, or weird, or that it would hold them back in life. Everyone's got that one thing they're obsessed with for absolutely no reason and the Scots language is mine. I knew if I was ever lucky enough to get published, I wanted to make sure the book I wrote was absolutely packed with Scots words and phrases because poetry is meant to be authentic, and I cannot be authentically me without the Scots language. If this is your first experience with Scots, I hope you have fun learning a bunch of new evocative, emotive, delicious words and phrases. If you're already a Scots speaker, or someone who has experience with Scots, I hope you connect with the language and enjoy what I've tried to do with it.

I'm sure this will sound incredibly clichéd, but when I was younger I always had a dream that one day I'd be able to write a book. I genuinely still can't quite believe this is all happening, and if this is all just a dream, I'd quite like to hit snooze a few more times if that's okay with you. I hope you enjoy this book, but if you don't, don't tell me: poets are sensitive.

Len Pennie, 2023

HONEY

Open the jar, honey, just let me try
to describe how my brain tells my body to die
for you, darling, baby, sweet angel, my love –
a cast-iron fist in a velvet-soft glove.
I know that you're gone but it hurts all the same,
the bruises have healed but I can't ease the pain
of knowing I let you, permitted, relented,
and the thoughts of your hands leave my body demented.
I'm haunted, by spirits poured slowly on rocks,
by incessant ticks of biological clocks,
but the taste on my tongue of your honey-sweet lies,
and the beat of my heart drowned in orchestral cries,
makes me laugh, honey.

My name became honey, something too fucking sweet,
and all that I am became something to eat,
to consume and use up, to be gorged and left bare,
and I begged you to stop, but you just didn't care.
You sucked on my bones, and you picked the meat clean,
and your fingers were gentle, and hurt like a dream;
but it felt, in a way that I can't quite describe,

like I was a banquet for you to imbibe,
And I'm starving, honey.

You called me honey though I said it pained me,
and day after day you bit down and you drained me,
of blood, of nectar, of hope, and desire,
and you opened the stove and threw me on the fire,
and I burned myself, honey, so brightly for you,
and I prayed that you'd fall in and burn with me too.
But you liked to watch me with intimate care,
as my flesh reached a succulent medium rare,
and I can't help but find it a little divine,
that my tears taste like beer and my ashes like wine;
and though you loved a drink you'd refuse just a taste,
you'd rather I rot into saccharine waste,
And I did, honey.

Now I have a name and it sure isn't honey,
and of things I could focus on, this one is funny,
cause it makes a cute metaphor, sticky and sweet,
and we can laugh about boyfriends and what they can 'eat',
but as with all things there's a little bit more,
there's you standing proudly and me on the floor,
and I can't wash you off, god knows that I've tried,
but when soap's been rinsed off and I'm all nice and dried,
it's still there, like honey's been poured on my skin,
and I know in my heart that I can't let you win,
But you have, honey.

THE CHILD

Your daughter asks why the boy punches her arm:
My dear, he's just flirty, it's part of his charm.
But it hurts, says the child, and it doesn't feel nice.
My dear, what is love without pain's bitter spice.
But he shouted says she, and he called me mean names:
My dear, that's love's chase, and it's all fun and games.
But I don't fancy him, and he won't leave me be.
My dear, just say 'thanks', now stop bothering me.

But since I responded he's much more invested:
My dear, say you're flattered that he's interested.
But he thinks since I thanked him that he should keep going:
My dear, that's your life now, you're better off knowing
Lest life's cyclical nightmare catch you unawares
In the playground, or bedroom,
He hurts cause he cares.

HAUNTIT

There's a ghost in ma heid, an A want it tae leave.
It isnae richt deid, but A'm wantin tae grieve
Fur the bodie it hurt till she startit tae want
Tae be the richt kind ae hollow fur ghosties tae haunt.

An A telt the hale truth tae the lad A wance lied tae;
Got hurt an fleed fae the boy A once cried tae;
Got burnt bi the man fur wham A held a caunle;
Slammed the door shut on hings A couldnae handle.
Cause a lie is a lie even when it feels real,
And aye, pain's gonnae hurt but it's somethin tae feel.

There's a lad lichtin fires wae matches he stole
Fae a lass eatin hauf tae it fills up her whole;
There's a man cookin meals wae food she cannae eat,
Then they'll fight an they'll shag till it wakes up the street.

Cause A didnae love ye, no cause love isnae real,
But the wiy ye held me isnae how love should feel,
It's the sick grinding ache ae ma flesh pierced by blades;
The king ae ma hert giein diamonds in spades.
When A'm drookit wae sweat fae the hings in ma dreams,

HAUNTIT

A'll can keep the lichts aff tae confuse laughs wae screams –
A game's no a game if ye cannae no lose,
An it's true, true love's hauns willnae gie ye a bruise.

There's a ghost in ma heid that A'd quite like tae kill,
An though he didnae love me, wan day somebdy will.
The cruel culmination ae thae twa painful years
wae a sweet exorcism ae saltwater tears
Taen the spirits fae graveyards they hauntit the most,
Noo A'm too fu ae life tae gie room tae a ghost.

THE DRAGON

Take me back to seventeen,
when I was whole and quite pristine,
and monsters lived in fairy tales and under beds,
but now you see they're holding court inside our heads;
An evil sexy wicked witch,
a psycho nutcase frigid bitch
began to dance,
and in her palm she held the power to entrance.

A hero fell upon his sword,
she hung upon his every word,
he held her tight enough that she might break,
the glittering imitative glint of gold so fake.
She loved and lost and hurt and bled,
and on her pain a dragon fed, and grew in strength,
the tendrils wrapping round her mind increased in length.

To slay the beast she took a pill,
which promised her that it would kill
the demon dead,
and yet he curled up, sleeping, still, inside her bed.
A dormant dragon, though asleep,

THE DRAGON

has claws which can inflict such deep,
unending pain,
and so our hero lies in wait to bleed again.
Proud empires fall and bad blood spills,
and even if my dragon kills
me in the end,
I'll curl myself around his scales and call him 'friend'.

It's been a year, I've changed my mind,
the dragon's really not the kind
of friend I want.
My life is more than empty crypts for ghosts to haunt.
I looked him in his scaly eye
and asked why he wants me to die;
and throwing back his head he loudly roared,
he told me dragons simply kill because they're bored.

Don't drag me back to seventeen,
when I thought I would be the queen,
so pure and sweet;
instead, I'd rather kingdoms knelt beneath my feet.
It's been a year of lies and fears;
through hope and heartbreak, blood and tears,
I found, in time, I run this ship; I rule this land.
If I'm to die by someone's hand,
it won't be mine.

VANITY

A beautiful woman who pleases the eye
Will be naught but a muse till the day she will die.
Beauty or brains, that's the choice that she will
Have to make or she sadly will choke on the pill
Made from guilt, and disgust, we will force her to swallow
A shell we carve out and then blame that it's hollow.
The painters and sculptors of days now long-dead
Would spend decades depicting each hair on the head
Of a woman they thought other men would find hot,
And then judge her for each single second she's not
Just prostrating herself before men she should thank,
Who use one hand to judge and the other to wank.
They will carve their initials, let fingerprints taint,
On their sexual fantasy rendered in paint,
The curves of a body just there to inspire,
A lifeless clay effigy, forged in the fire
Of sexist toxicity, cruel and sadistic,
An obsession whose object we'll call narcissistic,

A Pygmalion myth chased by those who can't stand
The thought of a woman not forged by their hand,
That cements the idea that society chooses

VANITY

The men to be artists, and women their muses.
So, make peace with frustrating, perpetual pain;
They will sculpt you a mirror, then label you vain.

IF A SHOULD DIE

If A happen tae die jist afore A can wake,
A pray that ma brain's gonnae gie me a break;
Sick ae bidin oan earth while A'm aye incomplete,
Haein rugs pult fae in ablow ma schauchelt feet.
A ken ye're giy scunnert wae ma constant moanin;
wid it kill ye tae gie me some sweet seratonin?
Cause A'm pauchelt fae thae contests oot ae ma league,
Gettin stuck in the vaccum ae manic fatigue,
An A cannae be arsed bein arsed wae ma life.
A've thoucht ae ma corpse mair than bein a wife,
Cause A dinnae hae dwams fu ae dresses an cake,
Mair efforts gone intae me plannin ma wake.
A'll gie yous a secret yous cannae staun hearin
It's no ma ain death that ma heid's ayewis fearin,
But the wiy they'd aw fun me, deid efter some time –
The corpse ae a lassie they aye thocht wis fine.
Rotten perfection, re-reversin psychology
A fankle ae sweet guilt an hyperapology.
Death doesnae scare me, A'm no feart ae dyin,
But A cannae staun bein the reason Mam's cryin.
If A bury masel, A'll feel safe in the soil,
befriend awe thae beasties that watch as A spoil

the gift ae a life A'm determined tae waste,
a meal A've sent back aifter merely a taste.
So, agin ma ain judgement, A'll droun ma ain sorra
An hope that A wake up less mental the morra;
An A hope thaim that love me can lairn tae forgive
That A wantit tae die afore A could jist live.
Ma mouth scrieves thae cheques that ma brain cannae fill –
Turns oot she's no quirky, just mentally ill.
A'm sorry ye're sorry A'm feelin this way,
A'll suppres ma distress till the point ye'll can say
She never gied panic an oot an oot cause,
Cause there wasnae a crisis wae her,
till there was.

OH, LOOK

Oh, look, the man that broke ma hert has somethin that he wants
Tae say tae me, the ghosts come back tae aw his favourite haunts.
He's done some searchin ae his soul an noo it seems he's seen
Jist how much pain his actions caused, and jist how cruel he's been.
A'm glad ye've found some peace at last, cause A'm no there jist yet,
A'm still reelin fae jist how audacious men can get.
So, noo ye've realised that ye were cruel an mean an rude,
Ye send me wan wee text an expect hings tae aw be 'good'?

Ye hink A'm gonnae read that an feel onyhin but sick?
That you've had an epiphany an seen that ye're a dick?
A'm no a bloody lesson, I'm no somethin that will tell
Ye how tae no pit lassies through the same sick kind ae hell.
An ye didnae want me writin hings, but ye're auld enough tae
    know it:
If ye didnae want the poetry, dinnae fuck over a poet.

A BODIE

Whit's a bodie tae dae wae the bodie they've got,
When the person inside feels lit somebdy they're not
Allowed tae exist as, permitted tae be,
When an act ae rebellion is sayin 'that's me';
When the bodie they hae doesnae match whit's inside,
When society tells ye ye're somethin tae hide?

An the guid women there wae a key in their haun
March ahint the locked gates an so proudly they staun;
If they'd jist wheesht a while then someday they might lairn,
There's mair tae ae lassie than whit they discern.
Whit's the point ae a movement that's stuck staundin static,
Knockin doon the glass ceiling an buildin an attic?

Whit's a bodie tae dae when their bodie's no theirs,
When the people in power catch us unawares,
An impose their ain laws that forbid us tae choose,
Whit we dae wae the rights they instruct us tae lose?
They gied us delusions ae haein a voice,
Then skelp us fur sayin 'ma bodie ma choice'.
They cannae be arsed wae bairns awready there,

They dinnae care much aboot weans needin care,
Aw they want is tae keep lassies quiet an smaw,
An then thank them fur lettin us exist at aw.

Whit's a bodie tae dae wae the bodie they've got,
When fur wantin tae lairn they git huckelt an shot?
An there's damn aw tae dae cause the people that should
Fix the problems they caused have decided they would
Rather sit oan their erses, an pat their ain backs,
But their regime ae power is showin its cracks,
An if they arenae careful we'll ask wan day soon,
Whit's a bodie tae dae except burn this shite doon.

OWERHINK

A owerhink hinkin A'm hinkin too much
Then owerhink hinkin again,
'Dae ye hink that A'm still owerhinking a touch?'
Comes the tortured eternal refrain.

Habits die harder than onyhin else,
Nothin's better tae kill than ma time
And if A could jist get oot ma ain bloody way
A could finally cry somethin mine.

The self-sabotage ae a brain stuck in flux
Bein feart ae the worst comin true,
The exhaustion ae sayin a wee bit too much
Maks me owerhink hinkin ae you.

A want it tae stop; A want it tae go.
A want fur jist wance tae be free
So it might help a bittie if A could jist know:
Dae ye owerhink hinkin ae me?
It's no that A'm wantin ye fashin aboot
The hings that ye say, dae or write,

But A hink it's jist helpful tae ken that A'm no
Oan ma ain agin aw ae this shite.

Dae ye get whit I'm tryin tae say tae ye noo?
A like ye, A want ye tae feel
Reassured that the hings that ma heid tends tae dae
Are cause ma brain makes fake hings real.

A'm a wee bit oan edge, cause ae hings in ma past;
People don't keep their side of the deal;
So jist gie me some time an A hope at lang last
A might hink a bit less, an jist feel.

LOVE AND HATE

I like you but I hate me,
so let's hang out and maybe see if I stop.
I'm so scared of hurting you
with pain that I've been fighting through,
but, darling, I'm not glass for you to drop.

I'd warn you off, tell you to run,
but, god, this flirting thing is fun,
and my heart knows you're not the one,
but you could be.
I've got tears, and you've got time,
and breaking hearts is not a crime,
but it should be.

I miss myself more than I miss him,
and you seem sweet and full of sin,
but the good kind.
And I've been hurt, and I've known pain,
and there's conflict seeping like a stain,
but enough about my mind.
Tonight, there's you, and you will do,

and I've told myself this through and through:
this one is kind.

I like you, and you love me,
but I will never truly see why you don't just run;
I'm always scared today's the day you'll see what lurks beyond the fun.

A love like mine is rare enough,
it's tinged with pain and awful stuff.
If you wanted blood and sacrifice, I could delve deep,
but if you don't mind, sweet simple soul, could we just sleep?

I can't promise I will dream of you,
I'll dream of him like I always do and cry his name,
but when I wake I'll find your arms and heal again.

I had you and thought I'd won,
thought healing arms and having fun were quite enough,
and I was done with love and hate.
But poyums are like fields unplowed;
a wedding dress can be a shroud
if words unsaid are spoke aloud,
so still I wait.

I don't hate you; I have no time
to waste on interests which decline.
I take my pain and make it rhyme.
And now I see – the one deserving of my love
was always me.

HINGS TAE MIND

There's mony hings ye tend tae mind as ye gang aboot yer day,
The hings they used tae dae tae ye or whit they used tae say;
A ken it feels lit bruises bloomin in ablow yer skin,
Unkind words an insults seem tae ripple fae within.

Ye're no quite sure jist how tae act or how yer hert should feel;
Ye arenae whit they done tae ye, their power isnae real;
An though ye cannae see it noo, wan day A hope ye find:
peace aye follaes ilka war, even wans focht ben yer mind.

A cannae promise cantie days, but pit yer armour oan,
Haud er forrit, keep the heid and min tae jist haud gaun.
Gin ye cannae hink ae hings tae say, or feel or even do;
Ae aw the hings tae mind the day, jist mind ye made it through.

IN MEMORIAM

They tried tae tak yer spirit, hen,
destroy that which they couldnae control;
So ye spak and the world didnae listen, hen,
smoort the smeddum that burned in yer soul.
Noo yer're deid but never gone, hen,
there's them that still carry yer name;
There's them that mind criminals bidin in courts,
heids that should hing heavy wae shame.
Auld Nick didnae ken ye fae Eve, hen,
ye hae but yer ain een tae see.
The wrang wasnae yours; the guilt was misplaced;
yer innocence plain as can be.
But they taen muckle mair than a life, hen,
a caunle snuffed oot in its prime;
A state-sanctioned murder ae innocent fowks,
punishment lackin a crime.
Yer soul's noo at peace wae the earth, hen,
sleep, and be wan wae the sky;
We'll scrieve yer name in books they cannae burn,
write a legacy never tae die.
But we willnae just beg ae yer pardon, hen,

those days have lang ceased tae exist;
We noo demand justice fur aw those lit you –
lang gone but eternally missed.

NOT ALL MEN

They tell us it's not all, but, god, it's too much
To be always afraid of the next creepy touch,
To be careful to not tell your trauma too loudly,
Lest you waken the *good men* just sitting there proudly.

But then suddenly here come the angels of fact,
Lives and innocence lost but his rep stays intact,
And they tell us we're crazy, hysterical girls,
But we googled how nails affect how a fist curls.

You must qualify nouns when you talk about men,
Or their pride might be bruised, and, my darling, what then?
And here come the experts to explain linguistics,
And we fail to take solace in morbid statistics;

Cause it might be, or will be, or already was,
and we know who is doing it, we know the cause.
We tell them our hopes, and our worst mortal fears,
We drown in a river of impotent tears;

And instead of a hand to pull us above water,
They say words to us that they'd hide from their daughter.

They pour in more liquid that's meant to dissolve,
Till we can placate, and stroke egos, absolve.

Because, yes, it's not you that would rape, bruise or kill,
But we told you who did, and yet somehow you still
Found a way you could centre yourself in our strife,
And she wasn't a daughter, a sister, a wife;

She wasn't just someone for someone to own,
She belonged to herself and had worth all alone.
And as tears dry and blood drips and bruises begin,
It's a game we don't enter and never can win.

Thank fuck it's the truth that it's some and not all,
And again 'not all men' comes the rallying call,
And we waste yet more time to refute points unsaid,
But that won't bring us back from the brink, or the dead.

CHATTIN SHITE

Awright, hen, hope you don't mind, A couldnae help but see
A conversation taking place that didnae involve me;
Never fear, sweet gentle lass, A'm here tae set that right,
Cause aw a lassie needs tae hear is a man there chattin shite.

Awright, doll, you're looking braw, I hope ye dinnae mind
A dash of impropriety in the guise ae bein kind;
For whit's a man supposed tae dae when blessed wae sic a sight,
It's physically impossible fur me tae no chat shite.

Here's a message tae the lads wha hink that I'm in need ae help:
Yer condescendin creepiness will earn yous aw a skelp;
Tell me a lassie cannae hink or speak or scrieve annaw,
And the ainly hing ye'll get fae me is a backhaun tae the jaw.

A'm no here as somehin cute fur you tae just abuse,
A'm the bloody artist, mate, I'm no the silent muse,
A cannae haud ma wheesht the now so tae avoid a fight,
Lads, tak heed fur aw wur sakes, refrain fae chattin shite.

LITTLE GIRLS

The little girl stands on a knife-covered ledge,
Dancing till blood starts to drip from its edge.
She's been licking her wounds since the first time she bled,
Getting judged for each thought she commits in her head.
She's been starving herself since she started to eat,
Connecting the dots of her heart's every beat.
She's been swimming from fishermen hiding their net,
And running from wolves that deny they're a threat.

And the men chime in, 'Silence girl, don't make a fuss,
I'd never do this, it's not all of us.'
To drown out her sorrow, the male chorus sings,
'It's only a few, you're imagining things.
You're making this issue seem worse than it is;
It was only a comment, a gesture, a kiss.
It was meant as a compliment – please take a joke,
Don't bite the hand groping you, savour each poke.'
And the girl learns the axis on which the world spins
Is powered by people who relish their sins.
So, she keeps her head down and she learns how to live,
To be quiet and not take much more than they give.
Cause the fragile knife edge she must constantly walk

Dictates every word she's permitted to talk,
Each mouthful is measured, each glance not too sly,
Lest she melt off her wings just from touching the sky.
And she'd love to exist as the person she knows
Lives inside of her mind, but her agony grows.

As she slowly but surely resigns herself to
Being smaller and using far less than they do,
Being meeker and not taking up too much space,
Being careful to always remember her place.
But the little girl vows that the curse will be broken,
She'll break down the barriers, leave them wide open:
For the daughters of little girls you wouldn't hear;
For the children of women you silenced with fear;
For our mothers we'll sing till the screams rip the air;
We are the little girls you couldn't scare.

DELUSIONS

Am I delusional, or just naïve,
That for once in my life I did truly believe,
That I'd found something better than I'd ever known
And I'd done all the therapy, truly had grown,
And worked on myself to the point that I could
Simply open my heart to the healthy, the good?
I practised each note I could fit on my score
Then I sang till I barely had lungs any more;
I gave till I couldn't take much more than breath
From a heart that was welcome to little but death.
And you came, then you left, and I don't think you meant
To barter with money you'd already spent,
But you were much kinder than I've ever had
And you gave so much good that it drowned out the bad.
For a few simple moments I started to hope
That my neck might be kissed by much more than a rope;
and that's the most dangerous part of it all,
In the sweet serendipity, simple and small,
In the moments of peace as we slept in my bed,
And I wasn't alone in the war with my head.
How stupid, how silly, how weak and naïve,

Was the girl that held you till we both did believe
That a moment so perfect could render us whole,
And could tame all the chaos outwith our control?
But morning must come, and perfection is just
A transient state like attraction and lust.
The sun rose on lovers and set on two parts
Of a whole that was less than the sum of our hearts,
And like every delusion we start to believe,
Hope without foresight was simply naïve.
And I'll do it again, cause it's just what I do,
And find someone who holds me much tighter than you,
Maybe they'll love me the way that I ought
To be loved, not just rented but finally bought,
And when I find the you that makes me into we,
I'll know what love feels like when given for free.
So call me delusional, call me naïve,
But love is the one lie I'll always believe.

TOO MUCH

I'm too much – too hard to handle;
I'm infernos; you want a candle.
I'm the rapids; you're a calm river;
I feel too much to last forever.

I burn too brightly; I blind your eyes;
I scream too loudly; I drown your cries.
I'm a tempest; you want light showers;
I am millennia; you're a few short hours.

I am on fire – a nuclear blaze,
I'll scatter your ashes in cities I raze.
My flames will lick bones, leave my enemies grieving;
If you can't stand the heat, then I recommend leaving.

And you thought I'd burn out, just a bright short-lived spark,
But I'm still on fire, and now you're in the dark.
My flame burns eternal, far away from your touch,
When compared with too little, enough's always too much.

STORYTIME

Let me gie ye a story that ye're gonnae love,
though ye've probably heard it afore,
Aw aboot this boy an the girl that he hurts,
because he wantit less ae her more.
It's aboot a girl an the boy that she hates,
because he couldnae lairn tae let go;
It's aboot a hert that wis simple tae break,
because love doesnae hear the word 'no'.
Let me gie ye a story, sit back an relax,
make believe that thae lies werenae said.
Let's play pretend that we pairtit as friends,
and A didnae wish you'd drop dead.
If we turn the tape backwards, flip it on its heid,
and scream till the truth runs tae hide,
Then it's Little Red's fault that she strayed fae the path,
and let the bad wolf come inside.
Let me gie ye a story ye're gonnae adore,
because you ayewis love when A cry.
A cuid try tae be sweet, spin ye some mair deceit,
but you cannae build lives oan a lie.
Noo it's lang aifter midnight, it's ma time tae bolt,
cause the magic's aw foosty an deid,

A'll gie true love's kiss a bit ae a miss,
cause A value ma hert an ma heid.
Noo A'm scunnert wae stories, we're no longer weans,
so the fairytale's lost its appeal,
Love's less ae a game when yer wounds hae a name,
an regret is aw A'm gonnae feel.
Thon muckle bad wolf's jist a scrappy wee dug,
an its barkin drives me roond the bend,
A'm so sick ae fables, they make me feel grim,
so A'm gantin tae skip tae the end.
So speakin ae stories, let me crack ma wee spine,
turn the page oan this sad fanklet tale,
An A gied ye a pairt ae ma tender wee hert,
but wae time, tears an love A'll be hale.
Ye didnae write me, pal, ma pages were fu,
ye jist couldnae decipher the leid;
We got lost in translation afore chapter two,
it's no ma fault ye cannae quite read.
Cover tae cover, A scoured each line,
then A placed you back up oan yer shelf,
cause heroes are fun, but when aw's read an done,
this princess can rescue herself.

MORNIN, FUCKER

Mornin, fucker, how'd ye sleep? I hope you're rested well;
I hope ye're catching quite the tan getting roasted red in hell.
I cannae tell ye all the things I'd like tae dae tae you,
Like punch ye till ye cannae move, or choke ye till yer blue.
I cannae tell ye anything cause that would break the law;
I'd dae hard time in any jail just tae break yer fuckin jaw.

Yer scum, ye dirty fuckin rat, I hope ye come tae ken,
That lassie-bashin twats like you are the very worst of men.
Ye see a lassie as a pawn in yer twisted fuckin game,
The maist shite ae aw this? A cannae gie yer name.
Fuck it, dickhead, this one's just for me and my ain mind,
And if A see yer face again, ye prick, A'll pay ye back in kind.
I'll make ye feel like sanity is something you should lose;
I'll shove ye doon ontae the flair and ye'll can start tae bruise.

I hope ye come tae terms wae whit yer conscience let ye do,
A hope tae god the next yin gets a better wan ae you.
The only thing that's kept me going, aw this fuckin time,
Is tae write doon aw the thoughts A hae and mak the fuckers rhyme.
A guess the thing that makes me feel like A am still complete:
Is every time you shoved me doon, A got back oan ma feet.

REFLECTIONS

Huv yous ony comprehension
Ae whit lassies huv tae face?
Fechtin tooth an nail
Tae gain respect in ilka space.

It's no aboot the hings A say
Or whit A try tae write,
It's the wiy A look while daein it –
Have ye ever heard such shite?

A lang fur days when A can talk
Wae makeup oan ma puss,
An no hae men enquire
How A've gone tae sic a fuss.

Or tell me how A turn them oan
Or whit they'd like tae dae,
Or redirect the dialogue
Tae whit they want tae say.

Don't get me wrang – A love the lads,
But feel that A should mention:

The fact A'm here tae educate,
No jist fur male attention.

An A'm telt every day
Tae keep ma heid doon and ignore,
But fur every 'gaun yersel hen',
There's a 'vapid ugly whore'.

So, A call oot the bastards
That mak ma work a game:
Haud a mirror tae misogyny
And watch it cringe in shame.

And tae the men so feart ae women
They cannae control,
Know while ye'll can brek a hert
Ye cannae break a soul.

Cause A'm hinkin ae quines scrievin
In their mither's mither tongue,
An lassies writin poetry,
The auld yins an the young.

Tae the wee girls, hear me say this,
In ma mammy's native speech:
Know that ye can advocate,
Inspire, craft an teach.

Ken yer words hae smeddum
Ahint the way ye look.
So, tak aw the keich life wheechs yer way
An fill a bloody book.

Dinnae listen tae thae fuds,
Keep daein whit ye're daein,
Make up a mind wae makeup oan,
Fur nae mind but yer ain.

IN THEIR OWN WORDS

'Men aren't as bad as she suggests'
'Please god, just let me see your breasts'
'Stop acting like it's 1950'
'Not all men are deeply shifty'
'Your image brings the lecher out'
'She's freshly waxed, I have no doubt'
'I'm picturing her giving head'
'I might be sixty, but I'm not dead'
'Can I just give your teeth a lick'
'That mouth's a waste not sucking dick'
'What's the Scottish word for "nice" and "cans"?'
'You were built by god to be a man's'
'She seems a right wee stuck-up cow'
'Please tell me why I'm hard right now?'
'You cause us to objectify you'
'And any self-respecting guy who
Sees you, needs to shoot his shot,
It's your own fault, you're just too hot'
'How much do you cost to bone?'
'I hope you know you'll die alone'
'She loves attention, she just feeds it'

'Someone breed the bitch, she needs it'
'If you say no I'd make you want it'
'You don't want comments? Just don't flaunt it'
'You ungrateful bitches give me rage'
'You're cute! hope you're not underage?'
'I want to fill you up with spunk'
'She's just a garage for my junk'
'I don't know why these whores persist'
'Misogyny doesn't exist'

And though it might seem quite absurd,
That I might take them at their word,
You see each line since I began,
Was sent right to me, by a man,
Then the opposite of consolation,
Comes without my provocation.
Someone will pipe up and then
Remind me that 'it's not all men' –
Congratulations, you win gold
For having once again just told
A woman screaming, caught on fire,
It wasn't you who lit the pyre:
You protest self-inflicted blame,
And all you do is fan the flame.

MEMENTO MORI

Kiss me in a graveyard as the sunlight bleeds to death;
Wrap your hands around my throat and swallow my last breath;
Drown me in your sorrows and paint all my colours black;
It's lonely by the ocean but at least the sea waves back.
I took a walk along the beach to plan my own demise;
The sky sang tortured descants for the waves to harmonise.
On quiet nights those harbour lights illuminate the pier,
I now know how the ocean feels when moonlight pulls it near.
I want you back inside me so this wound can never heal;
I only want to die so I can see how it might feel.
I want to taste your emptiness as it fills up my heart;
I crave the end so much I cannot wait for it to start.

I miss the pain inflicted when it's you that holds the knife,
Of all the things you took from me, why leave me with my life?
You wrapped me in my blood-stained sheets, a shroud fit for a queen;
I've scrubbed till my flesh sings for you and still my soul's unclean.
I've long since begged to stop this game for it's you who always wins;
I've come to crave the darkness for it covers up my sins.
I miss the days when kisses were all that you deigned to steal;
I want your ache to be the last thing that my soul will feel.
Come and find me laid within the crypt of our short-lived romance;

Let me take the hand that broke my heart and lead you in a dance.
We both ignored the bruises blooming raw beneath my skin;
You held my corpse so tenderly until the rot set in.
You stole a flower from my grave, made perfume from its bloom,
And now my soul's condemned to roam my desecrated tomb.
You erased the chalk-white outline where my mortal form once lay;
My devil's just an angel who's forgotten how to pray.
I've bled enough to know that tears will not remove the stain;
You've savoured every drop of hate that boils within my brain.
You burglarised this haunted house and made yourself at home,
And now I must commit myself to live a life alone.
I cannot bear the wretched numbness your absence imparts;
I'd sooner that you slit my throat than separate our hearts.
Give me tortured agony, a sweet eternal ache;
At least you'd have to hold me close to cause my heart to break.
Though wounds we have will heal in time and tears we weep
    will dry;
Memento mori, love of mine, remember: you must die.

THE LIBRARY

What if stories told us? What if books read us back?
Would we fill up the pages with things which we lack?
Could you construct your legend with things that you feel?
Could you make-believe fake till it starts to feel real?
Would you write about poverty, hunger and pain,
Droughts drowned in sunshine, and floods scorched by rain?
Could you sail on a shipwreck of paper and glue?
Imagine the tale if your story read you.

It's a curious thing, to be handed a book,
An infinite void into which one can look,
With pages unwritten and stories untold,
Pouring through chapters as yet to unfold.

But my library's burning; my books are ablaze,
The pages consumed will sustain it for days.
The moonlight recedes as the shelves turn to dust,
The oxidisation of knowledge and rust.
And the stories I told, that nobody remembers,
Transform tangible objects to transient embers.

The books that I filled with the things I once knew
Were lost to the lies that I swore became true;
And the singular blessing escaping that night
Was the hope that the wrongs were the type I could write.

So I sat at my typewriter, writing my wrongs,
And putting each book back where each book belongs.
And as each shelf was filled with the pages I chose,
Like the sunset in exile, my library rose.
And with each tome handcrafted, from paper to spine,
My library's open, and the stories are mine.
I own my own narrative, rewrite the start,
Delved inside the ashes and salvaged my heart.
And though far from idyllic, I do not intend
To abandon my book till I've written the end.

THE MOTHER

What is a mother if not the foundation
Upon which we can pour every drop of frustration?
The root that exists just to nurture the tree;
If her family is happy, who cares about she?
Who took seeds of her hope she decided to sow,
for to nurture them carefully safely to grow,
Into people exceeding her best expectations –
A life now defined by its own limitations.

If I have a daughter, I hope she'd forgive
Me inflicting the world within which she must live;
The labour demanded, the effort expected,
The agency that will be cruelly rejected.
Putting dead last, what was once the initial,
To render her body and joy sacrificial.
I think of my mother, in some other place,
The lines of sheer worry now etched on her face,
And imagine how different her life might just be;
And I weep for the woman who toiled making me,
Who risked her own death in creation of life,
To carry out duties of mother and wife;

May we meet and, as equals, regard one another,
And know you were a person before I called you mother.

HER

Try not to struggle, girl, don't make a fuss,
I'll tell you a secret now, just between us:
Please keep yourself silent, to make him feel loud,
To avoid seeming arrogant, stop feeling proud.
Don't turn your achievements to something they're not,
It isn't that special, you aren't that hot;
To gain some respect, simply cover your ass,
Your tits are on show, so you're lacking in class.
With makeup like that, who'd you think you're impressin?
Listen to us or we'll teach you a lesson.
Appease your detractors, but don't seek to pander;
Face critics with grace and just smile at the slander.
Be sexy, not slutty, not frigid, or rude,
Keep it in your pants, but mind don't be a prude.
When you're youthful, we'll shun you for being too young,
Cause there's nothing that's worse than a petty child's tongue.
But age past the point where the years now are shown,
And along with maturity, apathy's grown;
And you'll find our attention has started to wane,
No one cares for the thoughts in a bitter hag's brain.
But maybe there's more to her story than shame,
as perception we know is nine-tenths of the game.

HER

Is she arrogant or is she proud of herself?
Are you mad she's out winning while you're on the shelf?
Is she crazy or did you just mess with her head?
Would you rather she sucked on your ego instead?
Is she angry or did you just push her too far?
Do her tears remind you of inflicting each scar?
Is she broken or did you just hold her too tight?
Did you make her feel wrong just to make yourself right?
She's inadequate just to make you seem proficient;
She's not too much, you're just quite insufficient.
So, I'll tell you a secret you're better off knowing:
She's well past slowing down, so you'd better get going.
While you've shown complacency, she's become stronger;
mediocrity isn't enough any longer.
So, it's time to improve yourself, step up your game;
When this little girl's done, you'll remember her name.
So please give me your struggle, girl, make lots of fuss,
They'll just have to run faster, to keep up with us.

IN THE NAME AE THE WEE MAN

In the name ae the wee man, have ye lost yer heid?
Did the ghostie no lairn that he's better aff deid?
Ye claimed self-defence as a means ae attack,
how yer knife wis in pain when it came oot ma back.
Hurt people git hurt by the wee pricks lit you,
That cannae pit thought intae hings that they do.
An ye try tae crawl back the way aw beasties dae;
Git me up tae high doh wae yer bullshit that's, tae
A degree, so audacious, it's almost collegiate –
whit dae ye take me fur? Some kind ae eejit?
I dinnae want a poyum aboot how ye did me wrang,
Cannae staun yer insincerity when shoehorned in a sang.
I'm sorry that it hurts yer heart tae inflict so much pain,
I dinnae want yer tears cause I've git plenty ae ma ain.
Save yer empty words cause there's damn aw that you could say,
There's so much blood ablaw the bridge it's swept the hing away.
Ye're scum, ye're trash, ye're oot ma life, an never gettin back,
Dinnae let ma front door skelp ye where the wee man pit a crack.

OUROBOROS

Who are you to deny me my right to exist?
Who are you to take issue with men that I've kissed?
Who are you to control what I think, say and do?
Who am I when I'm finished pretending I'm you?

When I lie to myself, even I don't believe me;
I only exist when another perceives me.
Like the boy trying hard to convince his mum that
I'm not damaged, or broken, or worthless, or fat;
That my arms have grown strong from the burden I carry,
But I'm not the girl mothers want their son to marry.
I'm the woman they feared they would one day become –
A mangle of parts in the shape of their sum.

My future is constantly grieving because
There are flies on the corpse of the person I was.
And the buzz that they're making drills holes in my head
And convinces me I would be better off dead.
There's a man who thinks my soul is one he can save,
There's another who's just finished digging my grave,
And I'll lie there, a case now in search of its basket,
Like a beer, or a body, I'm made for the casket.

And I hate the girl he thinks that he knows,
Like a baby, or tumour, the fantasy grows.
I nurture it slowly with agony's moans;
It leaches my calcium, forming its bones;
It splits every cell and consumes what it wants –
Leaves the fuckable crater my poltergeist haunts.

And I hate it, this thing that pretends to be me,
It's pathetic and almost too cheap to be free;
The grotesquery youth once presented acclaim
Has been slowly dissolved by my infinite shame,

And I'm tired, but not quite enough to pass out,
And I'm angry, but slightly too scared to just shout,
And I'm hungry, but skinny tastes too fucking sweet,
So, I count broken pieces, find I'm incomplete.
Cause he took one and kept it and used it to fill,
The one part of him that I don't want to kill –
The hurt inner child, the epitome of
The scared little boy his own dad didn't love.

And I get it, but there's not a single excuse
That absolves an abuser of giving abuse:
Not the alcohol, drugs or the childhood or me;
Not your grief for the man that you thought you would be.
Who are you to think you can exist on my page,
As anything other than trauma and rage.
Who are you to think you're why my poyums draw breath?
You're a posthumous footnote, foreshadowing death;

OUROBOROS

You are trapped here; by my hand you'll never be free;
I am much worse than you, and you'll never be me.
This one ends as it started, like all sick things do,
A grotesque ouroboros stuck questioning you.

TECH SUPPORT

A hink A've caught a virus, an it's chaingin aw ma code,
The error message ben ma heid says its gonnae explode.
A hink A've git ma wires crossed; the numbers arenae guid,
The screen's gone blank, an digits arenae daein whit they should.

So, A telt ma pal that kens the hings A often cannae mind;
He sat wae me and helped me set ma phasers back tae 'kind'.
A asked him whit it said inside the wee error report:
He said, 'Aw that ye needed wis a wee bit tech support.'

Ye hae a team ahint ye, an they're workin aw the time,
Developin the updates fur tae build yer ain design.
An, aye, there's bugs an wires crossed, an hings ye cannae dae,
But life's a game that's meant fur mair than wan ae us tae play.

Ye cannae keep yer progress if ye dinnae save the file,
Jist gie the game a pause fur now, come back in a wee while.

Haud gaun, haud forrit, keep the heid, an try tae no forget:
Failin means yer playin, an the game's no ower yet.

YOURS

He said, 'Write me a poyum,' this boy that I knew;
I said, 'Break my heart first and I'll write about you.'
Cause I only write poyums for money or love,
And since neither are offered, I think I'll hold off.
Because poetry lives in the breaking of hearts,
The end of beginnings, the stopping of starts.
And you come to me? Expect me to provide
An externalisation of things kept inside?
So, I wrote you this poyum, you chaotic man;
Once I broke both our hearts the way only I can.
Cause I sometimes write poyums when struck by that spark
Of cold inspiration igniting the dark;
I wrote about chaos, and things left unsaid,
And the way what you say invokes peace in my head.
He said, 'Write me a poyum,' this boy that I knew,
I hope this one makes up for what I did to you.

THE LITTLE POYUM

So, I wrote this little poyum and things got out of control;
I found a voice outwith the page and sold ma bloody soul.
They paid me lots of money but it never felt enough,
So, I made my mind an island, and filled it full of stuff.
And let's not talk about the lads cause I dated quite a few,
Found something very close to love that was almost nearly true.
No one really stayed for long enough that they were mine,
My heart got broken once again and the poyums flowed like wine.
But still I've found, through all these years, one constant static thing,
Though sparkle holds a captive court, authenticity is king.
The more I hurt and break and bleed and lie and cheat and sin,
As long as I keep making art the crowds will listen in.
As long as I give something of myself for them to keep,
As long as things are nice and light and wounds are not too deep.
As long as inspiration burns its cauterising spark,
As long as poyums drip from lips that tremble in the dark.
As long as I can hold my head above the waves and scream,
I can't regret the little poyum that gave me my dream.

VIRGIN MARY

Virgin Mary, quite contrary, how can A no come inside?
The nicht's still young, let's hae some fun,
Ye dinnae hae much time tae bide.

Allow me tae sweep ye aff ae yer feet and wheech ye right intae
   ma bed;
Jist let me kiss and lick and fuck the thochts right oot ae yer head.
Ye arenae that young, and no quite that dumb enough that ye
   really retain
A naïve notion ae love as an ocean, are ye really that sick in the brain?

Forget childish beliefs that men are aw thiefs,
An that you present somethin tae steal;
Wipe thae tears fae yer eyes, hen, ye arenae a prize,
Ye're jist somethin pretty tae feel.

Sweet virgin Mary, it's really quite scary
How little ye ken ae yer soul;
Ye still hink a man will jist come alang and fill in the haufs ae
   yer whole.
Ye won't be content till yer time is aw spent, and yer cup has
   been drained till it's dried;

You're aw oot ae luck cause he jist wants tae fuck, now wouldn't
    you rather A'd lied?

Sweet virgin Mary, the world can be scary, for angels who never
    take flight;

Stop haudin oan to this pure image of you, and A'll keep ye
    warm fur the night.

Ma sweet darlin Mary, ye arnae contrary, it wasnae yer fault whit
    went oan:

He taen whit he taen, left his rot in yer brain, an by sunrise the
    bastard wis gone.

Ye're no less whole or pure, nor in need ae a cure, cause he
    didnae break mair than yer trust;

Tae yersel please be kind, an A pray that ye find, ye're worth mair
    tae a man than his lust.

Love shouldnae be rough, and it brings wae it stuff that at present
    yer brain cannae see,

An Mary, A pray that wan day that's the truth, cause it hasnae
    quite happened fur me.

YOU DON'T RHYME

Poetry's harder to write than you think;
Inspiration is fleeting and rare.
To sit down and pour out your heart on the page,
You need something about which you care.
I write as I live without structure or form,
Create poyums as dark as my brain;
I pick out some themes, intersperse them with dreams
And try to make art out of pain.
So, why do I struggle to write about you?
You don't really make much sense to me;
You're the moment of stillness before hell breaks loose –
A presence where absence should be.
How can someone callously care like you do,
Or silently drown out the dark.
You're the laughter that follows a tearful goodbye,
The kind word in a cutting remark.
You laugh when life hurts you; you smile when in pain;
And you frown when the light shines your way.
But when I see your face, things fall into place,
And I know just the right thing to say.
My heart writes you poems your ears will not hear,
Each word contradicting the last,

YOU DON'T RHYME

You give my heart reasons to hope against hope,
Forget pain which consumed poyums past.
So, my deafening mime, I do pray in time,
The words that I write will ring true,
And though it doesn't make much linguistical sense,
I hope that I might rhyme with you.

THE DOLL

Life isn't fun when you're seen as a toy
mishandled and undressed by some careless boy
removed from the box with a bit too much force
not allowed to complain as a matter of course
living life as a doll is much less than fantastic
first grossly mishandled then smothered with plastic
his brand-new and beautiful shiny new toy
who only exists when in sight of a boy
while he plays till her boundaries bend like elastic
he pretends that consent has been enthusiastic
and she's perfect, she's pretty, she's passive and meek
if you slap her the bitch will turn the other cheek
her limbs can all pose and her hair can be brushed
and she'll fuck you when asked and she never feels rushed
she never feels anything you don't dictate
she watches her manners, her temper, her weight
her hands can make dinner, hold makeup or cocks
she's never allowed to think outside her box
she endures yet another sick sleazy rude barb he
thinks is just a joke, like he thinks she's his barbie
and then little by little he starts to get bored

THE DOLL

then she'll lie there in silence, alone and ignored
there's a much newer model for him to enjoy
So discards his long suffering, once favourite toy
who now comes with accessories, trauma and shame
who no longer enjoys being part of his game
her smile starts to falter, her spark will now fade
at least dolls get to rest when they're done getting played

MANDEMIC

The world's kinda ending, and I'm all alone.
All I want is a cohesive plan,
Swiping through soulmates for one of my own:
My dystopian fictional man,
Maintaining his distance, two metres away,
While suspense puts me straight into hell.
He'd send me a text that would possibly say
You're even more hot IRL.
The ice caps are melting, but so is my heart;
There isn't much time, dear, so how bout we start
To develop this romance, outwith our two phones,
Replace notifications with laughter and moans.
The global pandemic won't impede our love,
You can still hold my hand through a surgical glove.
Is a little companionship too much to ask?
I don't mind if you kiss me while wearing a mask.
He'd rub his hand gently on my vaccine site;
Can we socially distance at dinner tonight?
It's hard to find love when you're in a pandemic,
And I want one that's sensitive, hot, academic;
I want one who's firing on every piston
With a sexy tight bod and a strong immune system.

MANDEMIC

More than anything else I'm just seeking a friend,
We can sit holding hands as we watch the world end.
He can tell me I'm pretty; I'll hug him and sigh
As the planet's engulfed and we both say goodbye.
You'll block out my sky like a solar eclipse,
Fall in love just in time for the apocalypse.

SELF-HELP

Guid news, lads, we've cracked the case, noo hear oor wee confession:
Some genius oan the internet has figured oot depression.
A ken it sounds a wee bit strange and giy hard tae believe
But when ye've never had it it's amazing what ye can achieve.
So wan day as A wallowed in a sad, depressive hole,
A state, mind you, of which we know A had complete control,
And even though A didnae hae the energy tae move,
A knew A had tae fix masel and fur wance an aw tae prove
That depression is a thing A chose, tae fix it's up tae me.
So, A taen his ancient sage advice and . . . made a cup ae tea.
Now maybe something didnae work because A did it wrang,
cause though A still felt weak as pish the tea was feelin strang;
Still undeterred, A heard some mair hings A can noo control;
A tain the dude's advice, ye see, and went on a wee stroll.
Now in his notes he didn't seem tae ken the reason why,
Despite all this good sound advice, A still might want tae die.
It's almost like, and hear me oot, cause this will blow yer mind –
Depression isnae sadness, and it's really no the kind
Ae thing that can be cured wae things like nature walks and tea,
And perhaps the person best equipped tae help masel is . . . me.
Like every other illness, of the body, mind or soul,
It's very much a case of something outwith oor control.

So tae geniuses on the internet that think that they know best,
A know yer only trying tae help but, please, gie it a rest.
A'm sick, A'm sad, ma mind is dark, ma thoughts are no sae nice,
But what A need fae you is empathy so, please, haud the advice.

CRAZY

Women are crazy and far too illogical,
It must be inherent, innate, biological.
Women have far more emotions than guys,
Because only a pussy just breaks down and cries.
So, we lie to our sons, tell them not to emote,
So, they hold in their joy, swallow lumps in their throat.
We convince them they're pillars of logic and reason,
So, there's not enough room for emotion to squeeze in.
But when he hurts his girlfriend, his friends will all say,
He's a really great guy, he's just had a bad day.

She pushed him to his limit; he pushed her to the floor,
She pushed all his buttons, so he pushed her some more.
Then here comes the passive to save him from hell:
From he shoved, she was pushed, she lost balance, she fell.

Emotion and logic cannot co-exist,
He shows one with his brain and the other his fist.
If she's upset, she's messy, feels nothing, she's cold,
So, she keeps it inside and she does what she's told.
A raised voice means hysterics, the fault of the womb,
So, she tempers her temper from cradle to tomb.

And learns how to handle the feelings of two,
To manage her own and her partner's heart too.
The biggest scam pulled is society's notion,
That anger from men doesn't count as emotion.
Paradoxical irony festers in ways he
Will scream in your face and then label you crazy.

NO TRUE SCOTSMAN

The real men don't catcall, or batter, or rape,
They clear the low bars under which they must scrape.
The only real men are the good men you see,
Because I'm a good man and he's nothing like me.

It wasn't a monster, cause they aren't real,
An intangible ghost isn't what she could feel.
It wasn't a boy; he was far too far grown,
But you just do not listen, ignore what you're shown.
You keep bad men separate from what you mean
When you talk about men, so you keep your hands clean.
No true man would do this, no real man would dare.
So, we'll keep chasing ghosts, hoping one day you'll care;
If we keep hunting monsters, we might be believed
Once we unmask the phantom he might be perceived.

As a real man, a true man, a man that exists,
Who used his real hatred, real cock or real fists,
And made a real woman feel real fear and terror;
He wasn't a fluke, or an outlying error,
And he hid in the shadows your words helped conceal,
When refusing to see that the bad men *are* real.

40 SECONDS

Put 40 seconds on the clock.
Who would choose misery? Who would choose pain?
If sunshine's an option, why would we choose rain?
We just want to be happy and healthy and free;
I just want to exist and let myself be me.
Yet something within me is making me cry –
There's a foot on my neck and a knife in my eye.
There's a black dog with jaws biting raw at my soul;
There's so much within me that I can't control.
And I just want to feel for a tiny wee while;
I just want to laugh and to dance and to smile.
And I'm so bloody lucky that you know my name,
Because there's so many people who can't say the same.
I'm telling you this for all our sakes,
It's one every 40 seconds that suicide takes.
And since you've been here reading, and I've sat and cried,
Another good person has just bloody died.
Stop the clock.

ANGELS

Dae ye still believe in angels? Dae ye hink there's something more,
Once we leave this mortal plane, might there be something else
   in store?
Dae ye hink the people that we love will meet us wance we've died?
When A gang tae see my nanny, will she mind the name A'm cried?
Cause the last time that A seen her, she couldnae mind ma name,
So, I like tae hink she'll smile at me an say she's free fae pain.
An sometimes when A'm sad A hink ae whit she'd mibbe say,
She'll tell me that she's seen me daein aw the hings A dae.
When times are dark A hink ae her, an ayeways end up knowin
That she'd be proud ae hings A've done – lit keepin masel goin.

If ma life ends afore A wake, A'm sorry that A didnae take
Twa seconds jist tae brush the thochts away.
I'm sorry that A didnae hear, the voice ae them that A haul dear,
An hink ae aw the reasons jist tae stay.

YOU'RE JUST A MAN

You are not heavenly, you're just a man, a soul within flesh, blood
and bone;
The gods gave me you as a means of control: I am Sisyphus, you
are my stone.
How many times did he hope against hope that this time the
gods would relent?
How many times did he scream to the skies, supplicate, pray, and
repent?

You are not royalty, you're just a man, a pauper who wants to be king;
You made me crave you as neck does a noose, a rope upon
which it could wring.
I am Ophelia, you are the lake within which I will take my last
breath;
A ministering angel I never shall be, the noblest mind wrought in
death.

We are not star-crossed; you're just a man, your house neither
noble nor fair;
Your tender caress feels like ice on my soul; how did you
convince me to care?

I am sweet Juliet, full of naïve regret, you are poison still wet on
my tongue;
Wherefore art thou, dear sweet love of mine? There is much of
our song left unsung.

I am the poet in control of her words, but your curse has left me
so tongue-tied,
The ink on my paper is all smudged with tears, and through
poetic verse I have cried.
You are not poetry, you're just a man, neither stanza, verse,
couplet nor line;
I did not write you, get the fuck off my page, there is nothing
about you that's mine.

AINCE UPON A TIME

Aince upon a time, or twa, in a kingdom far away,
Lived a lass who found a prince who said he couldnae stay.
He didnae want tae hurt her cause she really was giy sweet,
But he chose tae sweep her clean awa instead ae aff her feet.
He said that it was him no her and fell upon his sword,
A noble knight so full ae shite, who couldnae keep his word.

He gied her pish pertaining tae his lack ae want tae stay,
An said the hings a noble knight is aften wont tae say.
You'll find a prince mair capable ae giein ye a save,
But A'll aye be here if comfort is a hing yer soul might crave.
So back asleep the princess went, as if by some great trick,
Her finger poised for next time she'd receive another prick.

So, A'll leave yous wae a warnin, fur the princesses oot there,
There's nae deficit ae princes fur a noble maiden fair.
But dinnae lose yer heid fur every puss ye find disarmin,
Cause sometimes frogs are preferable compared wae prince
    uncharmin.
An dinnae fash, dear princesess, for your soulmate he wis not,
This prince wasnae yer ending: he wis filler fur yer plot.

So, ride intae yer sunset wae yer crown abune yer heid,
cause lookin back oan princes past,
A'd sooner ride their steed.

THE FEAR

Why are women so scared of a tiny amount
Of bad men, that's so small it's not worth the count?
Why can't they just accept that it's some and not all,
That the number of bad men is laughably small?
So, men laugh at our sorrow for something to do,
Cause its funny when women are scared that it's you
Who might turn out to hurt, or abuse, or control,
The wolf's a good guy till he swallows you whole.

It's just a bad apple, a bug in the codes,
But the orchard is rotting, the server explodes,
Embedding its shrapnel in all the good guys,
Who scream absolution to drown out the cries
Of the women they swear they would never cause pain.
So, they interrupt elegies just to explain:
I'm such a good guy, why are you acting crazy?
But cautious suspicion's not a game she plays. He
Just can't understand that the reason I'm scared
Is cause this time I've learned that I must be prepared.
Fear keeps me alive despite what bad men planned;
If you're such a good guy, surely you'll understand,
That your fear of rejection, or judgement, or scorn,

THE FEAR

Just cannot compare to the calluses worn,
Onto each individual cell of my terror,
That my death can result from one singular error.
If perpetual vigilance fails me, what then?
You won't hear our screams while you shout,
Not all men.

NOT ALL MEN 2:
TOO ALL TOO MEN

Won't someone please think of the good men out there?
Who would never hurt women and would never dare
To do anything other than treat them like queens –
He's such a wee saint that it's etched in his genes.
And yet women, those bitches, just want to be mates,
And our good saintly prince won't get asked out on dates,
So, he sits and he nurses the wrath that he's feeling,
And thinks not on what about Him's unappealing;
He deserves a text back; he's entitled to chances,
At sex and relationships, love and romances.
If only the women had much better taste,
They would all just pick him, and they would never waste
Their time on the men who would make them so sad,
Cause it's so bloody easy to know which guy's bad.
So, ladies, when hurt by abuse, cheats and lies,
spare a thought for the real victims: all the 'nice' guys.

THE MUSE

Gin A scrieved ye, they'd cry me a liar; gin A sung ye, A'd be telt
A'm wrang;

A poyum wid seem convolutit, an ye sure wouldnae fit in a sang.

Yer image wid bleed through ma canvas, an charcoal wid smudge
oan yer hert;

A cannae find words the way you can; A wouldnae ken whaur
tae stairt.

A sat doon tae scrieve ye a poyum, an A didnae ken whaur tae
begin,

Ye've scribbled aw ower ma sketchbook – maisterpiece wae the
lines coloured in.

The poetry breenged out ma coupon, the leid flew awa fae ma
tongue,

Cause A dinnae hae words tae describe ye; the wee sang ae oors
lies unsung.

A dinnae hae words fur a sonnet, when ye're here A ken not
whit tae say;

Ye're infinity aw in an instant, worth much mair than some auld,
cheap cliché.

A am bound by the words that A'm lackin; ma poyum's aw A hae
tae give,

But A cannae find words tae write ye, no lit you can mak poetry live.

And yer haunds craft sic beautiful music, and ye capture ma soul
in a sang,

Yer harmony played oan ma hertstrings, and ye write like ye've
never been wrang.

I hope ye enjoyed ma wee poyum; it's no much but it's aw that
A've got;

A could scrieve till aw words loose their meanins, dae ye justice
A simply could not.

So, A'll gie ma wee hert tae the paper, fill the page wae the
words that A choose,

Ye've inspired much mair than a poyum, noo ma smeddum cries
you its new muse.

SOLIDARITY

Aw the big high heid yins wae the power tae mak laws
Willnae feel the pain they cause as maist ae them hae baws.

They dinnae ken the awfy stress ae pishin oan the tests,
Boakin every time ye wake an beelin in yer breasts.

Mibbe ye're no ready or ye cannae thole the pain,
Wan ae mony reasons how ye dinnae want a wean.

An it's lang syne been the darg tholt bi the poor, the sick, the young,
the fate ae wham noo hings fae strings the high heid yins huv strung.

They gie the work tae ither fowks, sit back, claim the reward,
but disappear the second that it's time tae cut the cord.

There's a fundamental difference we see ilka day and night,
They can row oan tap ae waves while we wade through the shite.

AS THE FATHER OF A DAUGHTER

'As the father of a daughter' isn't saying what you mean,
it doesn't evoke hearts of gold and hands completely clean,
it tells me you define the progress that you make or show,
by the way that it impacts you and the people that you know.
It says 'now I've had a daughter I have finally decided,
I understand what hell is like now I am sat beside it'.

'As the father of a daughter' I wholeheartedly agree,
the patriarchy's run by men but somehow excludes me.
'As the father of a daughter' I am finally invested,
in making sure the bad men are all captured and arrested.
'As the father of a daughter' I am somehow still unwilling,
to see beyond the people who are raping, hurting, killing,
to the covert implication of the choices that I make,
to only care now I can see my interests are at stake.
'She is someone's mother, sister, daughter, friend or wife',
perpetually eulogised by people in her life,
Unable to exist outwith the men providing structures,
a picture that without the frame spontaneously ruptures.

'As the father of a daughter' please don't centre your involvement,
your proximity to women doesn't imply your absolvement.
Don't tell us the reason for your sudden change of heart;
don't tell us you had a kid and now it's time to start.
Acknowledge, see and mitigate the damage that it does,
to hear men say they didn't care till they had one of us,
Of all the things you tell your child, and everything you've taught her,
show her she has value, not just as her father's daughter.

BOYS WILL BE BOYS

Boys will be boys who'll be men soon enough,
And if all that we teach them is how to be tough,
They will learn the misguided ubiquitous notion
That anger is anything but an emotion.
We must teach them the strength in their vulnerability,
Show them a kind heart doesn't evoke fragility.
We must let our boys cry, let them vent, let them sing,
Let them sob and emote and feel every wee thing
That a human should know they can feel and express;
Remove all the rules on how they ought to dress.
Let them set their own boundaries, be hurt and forgive;
Let them see that toxicity's no way to live.

Boys will be boys who will one day be men,
And with respect and boundaries hopefully then,
They'll see 'no' as a sentence that's full and complete,
And not as a challenge that's there to be beat.
Teach them to care for both themselves and others,
Create standards to which they can then hold their brothers,
Love them without apology, fearless and loud,
So, our boys will be boys that will make us all proud.

CIVIL WAR

At ease, soldier, there's peace noo, at last.
She's jist a mistake ye can leave in yer past;
She's jist an error in yer flawless code;
She's jist a bomb; she wis built tae explode.

At ease, soldier, let's leave this war civil.
Ken A'm no guid wae details, but ye burnt lit the divil,
An ma heid's infiltratit wae enemy spies
I should mind that aw's fair noo in love, war, an lies.

At ease, soldier, it was aw in guid fun;
Atween your arms or bullets, jist gie me the gun
Wan mair day wae you or a lifetime in hell?
Gie me yer weapon, A'll dae it masel.

At ease, soldier, it's been ower a year,
And aw she minds ae you is the bruises an fear;
Aw she minds ae yer regime ae fear an control is
She called fur a truce afore she called the polis.

At ease, soldier, the war's long since deid,
And piece by piece peace is what's left in her heid,

An the shrapnel's still in there, but it's no quite as deep;
She still kens yer name but at least she can sleep.

Dear, she wha wis her an noo fechts tae be me,
The war won't be won till the day that ye dee.
Dear, she wha wis me an no fechts wars anew
Aye, he did win the war, but he cannae win you.

At ease, hen, ye're a soldier nae langer;
There's new wars tae fecht, but ye're aye gettin stanger;
Ye're aye in the sun noo ye've cut oot the shade;
Ye've gien yersel warpaint that's no gonnae fade;
Ye've pit oan yer armour an polished yer gun,
An aye there's still scars, but, ma darlin, we won.

THE GOOD OLD DAYS

These days women aren't worth the effort that men put
Into flirting, chasing, hunting, shooting
Shots we have to shoot.
They just do not appreciate that we are such good guys;
Instead, they offer friendship as a consolation prize,
Ungrateful women who don't know the kings that they're rejecting,
They shatter fragile egos that have taken years perfecting.

They aren't like the women from those golden good old days,
So full of grace and opioids, refined old-fashioned ways.
In days gone by they'd cook and clean, raise kids without the bitchin –
They'd be barefoot and medicated, pregnant in the kitchen.
In days gone by, men could be men and without too much strife,
Transition from their mother's house to one run by their wife.
These days are in the past, dear boys, and there they will remain –
what seemed a smile in hindsight was a grimace fuelled by pain.
For too long mediocrity has been unduly praised;
I hate to burst your bubble, but the bar has now been raised.
Those 'good old days' are long gone, we no longer have to settle,
We now can be discerning and have ways to test your mettle.
It isn't good enough to exude toxic masculinity,
You'll find that fewer women will now frequent your vicinity.

Consider it a simple case of market saturation,
Please desist your mediocre ego masturbation.
So, lads, you're absolutely right: stay home, don't try to mingle,
Then they'll believe you when you say
It's your choice that you're single.

AM I REAL?

Am I real?
Do I exist?
If I died now, would I be missed by more than Mum?
If the sunrise burns my smothered voice,
Would angels praise me for the choice to leave wars left unwon?
I think I'm real;
I do exist,
The monsters back and he is pissed,
He wants my head,
Do you understand I want to live *and* to be dead?

Am I real?
Do I exist?
I do not think the mouths I've kissed curved in a smile,
So, I'll lie down perchance to dream,
Perchance to float through tears which stream, and rest a while.
I like my life, I like the taste
Of having time I shouldn't waste,
But I can't tell if leaving now would be forgiven,
Eternal bliss in endless heaven, or lifetimes spent in hell.

I know I'm real,
I do exist,
So, I'll sit down and make a list of reasons why
And read one out each time my brain tells me the lie
That I'm not real, I don't exist.
The thoughts are there, and they persist,
but so do I.

DEAR DARLIN

Dear darlin, should this letter find ye' lang after A've passed,
Please ken ma heart still loves ye, though it may huv beat its last.
Wae every gasp a hud inside the body lang since deid,
Ken each breath wis meant fur you, each lungfu freely gied.
Ken you wur wance the lassie that belanged under ma airm,
A lassie that I'd fecht tae keep fae ony kind ae hairm,
wha held each moment tenderly wae a heart abuin them aw,
An fur a time ye wur ma lassie, an A wis yers annaw.

A cannae owerstate this, but A'll gie it a wee go.
A'll tell ye how ye mak me want tae live a lang life slow.
A'll tell ye ae the way yer heart made mine ken whit love is;
A'll tell ye there's no life A want that doesnae contain us.
There isnae only force abuin this earth that hus power left tae
    smite us,
An if there's better aifter life, it's cause it'll reunite us.

The light that shines ahint yer een,
The lips lies seldom rest atween,
The heart A'll haud as lang as a hae breath,
Come cruel cauld blade an smite ma neck – love kens nae death.

This lassie's lassie will be fine,
A ken fine weel ye'll hae the time tae love anew,
But mind, ma dear, when there wis us, an we, an me, an you.

NARRATIVES

I'm telling my story, it's mine after all,
and this masterpiece won't write itself.
What started as tragedy turned into hope,
The weight of which buckles the shelf.
I put I into life and then life into me,
As I reconstruct what was once gone,
I stoked every ember my heart could remember,
And I nourished the flames till they shone.
I wrote down the things I now have in my life,
and I found that from heartache and pain,
I took strength and resilience, a beautiful brilliance,
And wrote pride where there once scribbled shame.
And I have done more than just simply get by,
So much more than escape or survive,
Through the galvanisation of love, time and patience,
I'll take hold of my story and thrive.
After life that was seldom what life ought to be,
Through laughter and love I'll be whole,
This story is mine from the cover to spine,
And the narrative I will control.

THE YEAR A SHOULDNAE HAE HUD

Can yous len me yer ears fur a toty wee sec, till A gie yous a
story ae mine.
It isnae ower long and A promise tae skip aw the pairts that wur
there tae fill time,
but A feel lit as Christmas and Hogmanay's ower and we've aw
just went back tae bein sad,
A should share wae you aw ma thochts oan a year that A
honestly shouldnae hae hud.

At the start ae the year, as days were giy dark and the shadows
were aw A could see,
A thocht tae masel, as mony ae us did, that life didnae haud
mair fur me;
A gied up, surrendered, let go ae the rope and forgot wha it is
that A was;
there's no braw wee way tae describe how A felt, but there's
millions ae people lit us.

Thon feelin is darkness and numbness and guilt, sympathetic tae
apathy's cause,

it's fechtin wae black dugs yer're wantin tae win, lyin doon tae be
   caught in their jaws;
but haud on, A'm here, A'm alive just aboot, and A dinnae intend
   tae be deid;
A'll fecht ma way through, the same way as you, and dae battle
   each day wae ma heid.

Noo A'm no religious but just on the off chance the wee man is
   bidin up there,
here's a wee plea fae me fur aw ae thaim lit us, a depressed wee
   atheist's prayer.
Mate, gie us a haun up oot ae this mess, gie us a totty headstart,
gie us a second tae catch wur breath and regain control ae wur hert.
Ken A'd love if A could relax, sleep and smile, tak care ae masel
   and eat,
A dinnae want much fur A'm easily pleased, and ma heart's quite
   content jus tae beat.

So, fur abdy listenin, wha kens how A feel, and bides in the dark-
   ness wae me,
wae wan year ahint us we look tae the next and dinnae ken aw
   that we see,
but you just lit me survived aw the hings that life tried tae tak
   and turn bad,
A pray that A'll see yous aw next Hogmanay, another year that
   we shouldnae hae hud.
A said this aw last year, A'm back wance again cause A fun ma
   way through wan mair year;

an, aye, it wis difficult, painful an lang, an it gied me the boak an
the fear;
A lost some great people, A miss them each day an A'll ayewis
hae ma ain regret,
but as Papa would say if he seen me the day, it'll aw work its ain
self oot, pet.

So, A'll see yous aw next year; A promise yous this, just the same
way as day follaes night,
we'll see yin another, jist twa broukit bairns, held thegither wae
duct tape an spite.

WHEESHT

Wheesht! They telt me, wheesht the noo, an dinnae mak a fuss,
Ye dinnae spik the wiy we dae, ye'll ne'er be wan ae us;
Sort thon verbs oot fae the nouns, pit them where they aught tae be.
So, upon ma tongue the silence hung, an the wheesht hel ontae me.

They telt me that tae chainge the world wis a war ne'er tae be won
Through ma ain choice a smoort ma voice an let the wheesht
    haud oan.
Gin ye cannae thole the dark an the sky abuin ye's black,
Haud yer wheesht fur lang enough an the wheesht will haud ye back.

Ye hae a vyce outwith yer gub if ye can jist believe it,
There's a poyum in yer heid the now that's ayeways wantin scrievit.
So scrieve till aw the ink gangs dry and yer haun burns lit thon sun,
There's time enough tae haud yer wheesht when aw the scrievin's
    done.
So dinnae fash aboot thon snash an aw the lies they tell,
Jist haud oan tae where ye're gaun, an the wheesht can haud itsel.

THE ART OF REJECTION

Let's all teach our daughters the art of rejection,
So they can deflect all that misplaced affection.
Sadly a headshake won't make him discard her,
If she thanks him, or laughs, that will make him try harder.
They can't be too loud or they'll anger the man;
They can't just say 'no', that's not part of his plan;
He sees 'no' as convince me, precursor to 'yes';
If she didn't want bothered, why'd she pick that dress?

Let's spare girls the lesson and just teach our boys
That women are people, not shaggable toys,
That 'no' is a sentence that's full on its own,
And once it is uttered to leave her alone.
Do not stalk her, or kill her, or cause her to cry,
Do not tell her you're truly a really nice guy,
Cause the nicest of guys just take no for an answer,
They don't stick around just in case there's a chance her
Mind will be changed, or you'll break her resolve,
Her 'no' is no puzzle you should try to solve;
She is not there to handle your random erection,
It's not girls who need teaching the art of rejection.

THE PRAYER

Dear God, there must be some mistake,
Your sacred laws I did not break; in fact, you see,
I added some, and thought you'd say
If you had seen the world today, that you agree.

I know not why you make me dwell
In this eternal burning hell, for I am good,
My actions, God, have surely been misunderstood.

Dear Lord, I took thy own advice,
And spent my mortal time on nice and kind endeavour.
Dear Lord, as thou knows oh so well,
For my good work I ought to dwell in paradise forever.

Though you said naught of being trans,
Of women being under man's restrictive hand,
Upon myself I took the task,
Despite not stopping once to ask what you had planned.
I am but man, yet I devise
My own interpretation wise of your great word:
For marriage held between two guys, despite their love before my
    eyes, oh, how absurd.

Dear Lord, I cast them from the flock,

Their lifestyle I decide to mock, for I know best,

Your teachings I have followed well, but I now find myself in hell
with all the rest.

I see that I haven't listened, abandoned those that we had chris-
tened, and cast them out,

In your own image they were made.

I now see I have disobeyed, so now I shout:

Forgive me for the sins I brought;

The lives of others I once wrought, the hubris of a mortal man

Who questioned judgement so divine,

Who placed your teachings after mine,

Was focused most on judging those I ought to love,

Now each of them resides forever, far above.

THE FIRST TIME

The first time that you kissed me was the first time I'd been kissed,
I couldn't help but wonder how much joy my life had missed;
To go through life with lips untouched till you swept me away,
Felt almost like I'd stayed inside on every sunny day.

The first time that you shoved me was the first time I'd been shoved;
Being hurt by someone stings much more when it's the one you
   loved.
You cried and told me it was nothing more than a mistake,
So, I held you close, adjusting how much violence I could take.

Acid rain dissolving statues isn't sentimental;
Damage goes unnoticed when it's slow and incremental.
The gradual increase of pain through things both done and said;
The frog in boiling water doesn't notice till it's dead.

There is a need within you love alone cannot provide
A rot that to eradicate I wasn't qualified,
I didn't leave to hurt you; I just couldn't stay much longer;
I stayed with you too long for love, but left for love much stronger.

BON APPÉTIT

You are cake and sweets and ice cream;
You are chocolate, lemonade;
You are mince and tatties, nutrients
A form expertly made.
The physical reflection of a spirit living free,
Every curve follows the blueprint
Of who you were meant to be;
Each spoonful a reminder that you're worthy of self-care,
Every stretch mark tells the story of a life that's blessed with wear.
Serve a smile with every meal and have a second serving
Of nourishment and sustenance – your body is deserving.
The value of replenishment cannot be overstated;
If cuisine be the food of love, then eat till your heart's sated.
Instead of numbers, focus on the pleasure you accrue:
Nothing will look better than a fully nourished you.

ADAM AND STEVE

Adam and Steve in the garden one day
Were embracing when suddenly Steve turned to say,
I've been told that by loving each other we're sinning,
But if god hates our love, why do we keep on winning?
Why have we been so blessed by the one who they say,
Thinks the love that we feel means we've wandered astray?
What's wrong, just do as the good lord has taught?
To love one another as we really ought:
To be loved without prejudice, judgement or shame,
To find someone whose soul, mind and heart are the same?

With a palm on his cheek, Adam gave his reply:
If living means leaving, I'd much sooner die,
Than to spend just one moment alone, or apart,
From the one who inspires each beat of my heart.
And it's yours for as long as you wish it to be,
I'm much more myself in the moments where we
Can be with each other in comfortable bliss,
How lucky we are to have someone to miss.
Let them burn down the garden and lock heaven's gate,
If the thought of such love can inspire their hate,

Then as god is my witness my judge and my guide,
Let him open my heart and observe joy inside;
After darkness and water and heaven above,
On the day he made you he said, 'Let there be love.'

COORIE

coorie intae me, ma love, dinnae heed thae yins
that dinnae care tae ken wur minds, an see love's acts as sins;
coorie fur protection, fae a warld that wants tae hairm
that cannae staun tae see a lassie haud her lassie's airm.
coorie doon tae sleep, ma love, A'll haud watch the nicht
tae haud aff ilka sneer an taunt an keep them fae yer sicht.
coorie doon, ma darlin, let the warld wheech aw it's snash,
A'll keep ye happit in ma hert, ma love, noo dinnae fash.
we hae a love worth fechtin fur, sic joy A cannae hide,
so, coorie doon wae me, ma love, ma jo, ma greatest pride.

ADDRESS TAE THE LEID

Fair fa your honest, sonsie face,
wha hinks ae Scots as a disgrace!
A leid that's meant fur lesser hings,
No there tae lairn:
A leid well-kent by mony fowk
That does nae hairm.
Ahint keyboards the wee troll hides;
Abuin yer soul the hatred bides;
Yer words are nocht but draps ae rain
Agin ma heid,
Taks mair than dubs aw filled wae pish
Tae droon me deid.
We ken the rot yer souls contain,
Wan single leid within yer brain;
A look upon ye filled wae shame,
But dinnae fash,
The Scots leid maun strive oan in spite,
Ae aw yer snash.
Then, word fur word, Scots willnae dee:
Ma time and tongue aw A can gie,
And gie it aw A will until ma final breath.
Oor poyums will be said by bairns

Lang past wur death
Is there that troll wha sneers in shame,
Or cries me mony a hatefu name,
Or *seeks tae cause me muckle pain*
Fur whit A dae,
Looks down wae sneering, scornfu view
On whit A say?
Poor devil! See him ower his screen,
His grammar neat, his English clean,
He fechts fur country an fur queen,
But doesnae see —
If abdy's gonnae look his way,
It isnae me!
But mark the chiels wha speak the leid,
Wha ken it's livin, never deid,
An ken it's fit fur aw the time,
No special days;
An sees the puir wee hypocrites,
Oan 25ths and Hogmanays.
Ye Pow'rs wha're wae me every hoor,
Gie me smeddum that ye cannae smoor,
Auld Scotland wants nae linguaphobes
Wae a hatefu heid;
But, if ye wish her gratefu' prayer,
Follae ma leid.

THE PERFECT VICTIM

Hi, I'm the perfect victim, and before you speculate,
I wouldn't even dream of going walking when it's late;
I wouldn't take a bus, or taxi, train or car alone;
I'd never make my way to work without a chaperone;
I fought back, but not too hard, just enough to gain your pity.
I'm plain in face and politics, not the kind you'd call too pretty,
I did everything that one should do and say and be;
NO, wait, if you could stop advising things like: well, if she
Had only been suspicious of the man from number ten;
If she hadn't listened closely when we shouted not all men;
If she hadn't worn that underwear under clothes that she was wearing;
If she hadn't smiled flirtatiously at men that she caught staring;
We weren't there, we didn't see, but we know she must have been
Doing something to attract attention, something so obscene.
Oh, shit, she's dead, let's backtrack so nobody can forget her
Ways she made herself a target, and should really have done better.

Hi, I'm the perfect victim – I'm nothing but a lie;
We've already done what will be used against us when we die.

CONTRADICTIONS

I am the kingdom which you couldn't rule,
yet you clamoured to make it your home.

I am the fire which you couldn't fuel,
yet you begged for my flames on your bones.

I am the lion which you couldn't tame,
yet you yearned for my teeth on your neck.

I am the one that you swore was to blame,
but it's your ship that caused mine to wreck.

On the canvas I bled like a gunshot,
hanged myself from the lines of your stave.

The fire singed clouds of a sunset
burning through that which you sought to save.

My love's a tempest of embers;
your love is rot and decay.

And that which I'll always remember is:
you couldn't force me to stay.

I'M NO HAVIN CHILDREN

I'm no *havin children*, A'm gonnae hae weans;
an ye'll can ask whit A cry them, no *what are their names*;
an they'll be gettin a piece, no a wee *packed lunch*;
an they'll be haein a scran, no *having a munch*;
they'll fanny aboot, they willnae *waste time*,
an when they scrieve their wee poyums, A'll mak sure they rhyme.

A'm no *havin children*, A'm gonnae hae weans,
who'll be gowpin an bealin when they've goat *aches* an *pains*;
an instead of *don't worry*, A'll say dinnae fash;
instead of *stand your ground*, dinnae take any snash;
ma weans'll be crabbit, no *in a bad mood*;
and they'll greet, no *cry*, when their day isnae good.

A'm no *havin children*, A'm gonnae hae weans,
wae a prood ancient language crammed in their wee brains;
an whenever life tells them their *English is bad*,
A'll tell them the hassles that their mammy had,
an A'll say ma maw's words till the day that A'm deid:
Ye'll be awright, hen, ye've a guid Scots tongue in yer heid.

Acknowledgements

I'd like to thank my big sister, Heather, whose strength, grace and willingness to learn and to grow no matter what life throws at her is a constant source of inspiration. My wee brother, Greg, whose seemingly endless well of patience, kindness and talent is a source of pride and envy in equal measure. My mum, who was the first person to hear the first poyum and will always be the first person I think about when I write. And to my dad, who takes credit for my sense of humour when he should instead credit himself with inspiring my tenacity and desire to fight for the people I love. Nanny, I'm only going to show you the happy bits of this book, and I hope you enjoy them.

I wish more than anything that my papas, James and Bert, and my nanny, Jean, could've seen what I've tried to do with the tools they gave me.

Thanks to my friends for holding me together, and lifting me up.

III

To Ludo, my agent, I am extremely grateful for the way you are able to translate what I say into what I mean. I will always be thankful to Eve White and Canongate for taking a chance on me.

I'd like to offer my eternal gratitude to Melanie, Fife Woman's Aid, Kate, Amanda, Action Against Stalking, Valerie and the counselling team at St Andrews University. These women helped me to rebuild myself, and I would not be here without them. Last in these acknowledgements, but always first in my heart, I would like to offer my solidarity, my undying respect and my unwavering support to all those experiencing or affected by abuse or stalking. There is help, there is a way out, and there is a future for you.

This feels like I'm writing a will, which I guess is accurate in some ways. I am not the same person I was when I started *Poyums*, the naïve, innocent, childlike version of me replete with endless optimism is no longer here, but that's okay. The current version is significantly harder to kill.

My last thanks are to you, the person engaging with my work. I appreciate you, and I hope you cry less reading this book than I did writing it.

An Interview with the Author

How important is humour in your poetry? How do you so successfully balance it with heavy topics like misogyny and mental health?

If I don't laugh, I'll cry. I think it's easier for me to deal with certain things by finding humour in them; it provides some distance, a wee interstitial space for me to sit in and avoid or deal with things as I choose. Life is sometimes sad and often scary. I like being able to play with those feelings in a way that takes some of the sting away.

In 'You Don't Rhyme' you write that 'Inspiration is fleeting and rare'. What, or who, inspires your writing most?

My biggest inspiration in life is spite. It's a functionally infinite, endlessly renewable resource for me. I don't say this flippantly.

I have often been told I have no power to make change in this world, and in spite of this, I intend to try. Spite the doubters, spite the haters, spite your wavering hope, your trembling lip, your shaking hands. Spite will see you right.

Why is writing in Scots so important to you?

It would feel weird not to use Scots in my work, it's the language of my internal voice and *poyums* is an externalisation of that. My family made sure I had a good Scots tongue in my head and I hope I've used it as effectively as possible.

There's a diverse mix of poetic structure in this collection. What is your favourite form of poem to write, and why? Prosaic, or more structured?

My poetry is the only thing in my life with any kind of structure. I like having wee parameters within which to work, and I like the challenge of finding the rhyme. I'm first and foremost a performance poet, and having that rhythm and rhyme is really important to me. I also like having a juxtaposition of these themes which are uncontrollable and uncontainable trapped in the confines of tight wee rhyme. Feels like a prison for the things I don't like and a hug for the ones I do.

Many of your poems discuss how writing has helped you through hard times. Can you tell us when you first started writing poetry?

I started writing poetry because I wanted something to focus on in times of extreme emotion. My biggest fear in life is being forgotten, and I really want to leave more than tears behind me when I go. I really hope *poyums* makes people feel less alone when they read it, or even just makes them feel something.

How does your Scottish identity overlap with your feminism?

My Scottishness and my feminism are intrinsically linked. I recognise both the progress and the prejudice of modern Scotland – we have much to celebrate in the former and much to work on with the latter. I want to see equality: of gender, of race, of sexuality, of ability, both in and outwith Scotland, and I want to continue to ensure my work is as intersectional as possible to help realise that goal.

Death is a recurring theme in your work, and on one level this collection is about living on in spite of suffering. To what extent is this juxtaposition of death and triumph deliberate?

I had a really bad fear of death when I was younger; I used to lie awake at night and worry that if I fell asleep either I or someone I loved would die. Then when I was a bit older, I struggled a lot with suicidal ideation, which is kinda the opposite side of a really shite coin you can't even spend. Death is never far from my thoughts, whether as a worry or a wish, and I think the best antidote to that is to make life as liveable as possible.

In your acknowledgements you mention that you aren't the same person after writing this book as you were when you started. How and why did this process change you?

The first poyum in this collection was written shortly after I left an abusive situation, and the final additions were being made as legal proceedings concluded three years later. It would be disingenuous of me to portray this collection as anything other than an *attempt* at healing, it's definitely not an entire journey, but it feels like the beginning of one. In truth, I think I'll be working on feeling whole again for many years to come. Not too many years, I hope.

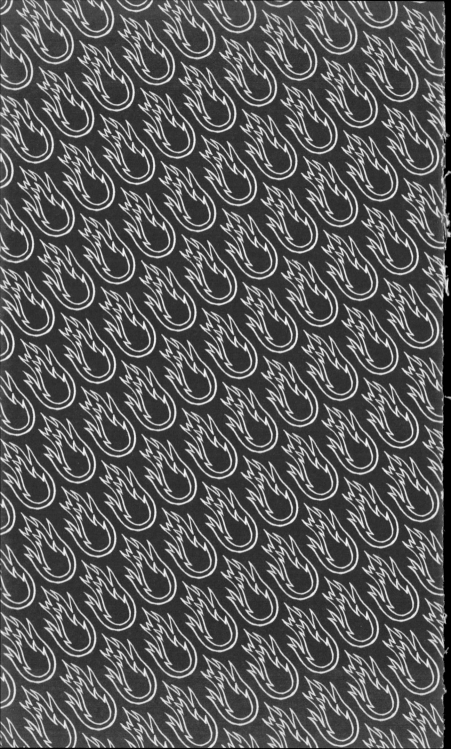